# REFLECTIONS
### FOR
## **LENT** 2017

# REFLECTIONS
## FOR
# LENT

1 March – 15 April 2017

JEFF ASTLEY
HELEN-ANN HARTLEY
GRAHAM JAMES
LIBBY LANE

with an introduction by
SAMUEL WELLS

Church House Publishing
Church House
Great Smith Street
London SW1P 3AZ

ISBN 978 1 78140 004 3

Published 2016 by Church House Publishing

Liturgical editor: Peter Moger
Series editor: Hugh Hillyard-Parker
Designed and typeset by Hugh Hillyard-Parker
Copy edited by: Ros Connelly
Printed by CPI Group (UK) Ltd, Croydon CR0 4YY

What do you think of *Reflections for Daily Prayer*?

We'd love to hear from you – simply email us at

**publishing@churchofengland.org**

or write to us at

Church House Publishing, Church House,
Great Smith Street, London SW1P 3AZ.

Visit **www.dailyprayer.org.uk** for more
information on the *Reflections* series, ordering
and subscriptions.

# Contents

# About the authors

**Jeff Astley** is an Anglican priest, and currently Alister Hardy Professor of Religious and Spiritual Experience, Glyndŵr University, Wales, and an honorary professor at Durham University and York St John University.

**Stephen Cottrell** is the Bishop of Chelmsford. Before this he was Bishop of Reading and has worked in parishes in London, Chichester, and Huddersfield and as Pastor of Peterborough Cathedral. He is a well-known writer and speaker on evangelism, spirituality and catechesis.

**Helen-Ann Hartley** is the 7th Bishop of Waikato in the Diocese of Waikato and Taranaki, New Zealand. Before that she was Dean at the College of St John the Evangelist in Auckland, New Zealand. She was ordained deacon and priest in the Diocese of Oxford and served as Director of Biblical Studies at Ripon College Cuddesdon.

**Graham James** has been Bishop of Norwich since 1999. Previously he was Bishop of St Germans in his native Cornwall and Chaplain to the Archbishop of Canterbury. He has served on the House of Lords Select Committee on Communications, and remains the Church of England's lead spokesperson on media issues. He has been a regular contributor to BBC Radio 4's 'Thought for the Day'.

**Libby Lane** is Bishop of Stockport in the Diocese of Chester. In 2015 she was consecrated as the Church of England's first woman bishop. She chairs the Diocesan Board of Education, and the Foxhill Diocesan Retreat House Committee. She is an elected Suffragan in the House of Bishops, Chair of Cranmer Hall Theological College Committee and nominated Vice Chair of The Children's Society.

**John Pritchard** retired as Bishop of Oxford in 2014. Prior to that he was Bishop of Jarrow, Archdeacon of Canterbury and Warden of Cranmer Hall, Durham. His only ambition was to be a vicar, which he was in Taunton for eight happy years. He enjoys armchair sport, walking, reading, music, theatre and recovering.

**Samuel Wells** is Vicar of St Martin in the Fields, London, and Visiting Professor of Christian Ethics at King's College, London. He is the author of a number of acclaimed books, including *What Anglicans Believe, Crafting Prayers for Public Worship* and *Learning to Dream Again*. He was formerly Dean of the Chapel and Research Professor of Christian Ethics at Duke University, North Carolina.

## About *Reflections for Lent*

Based on the *Common Worship Lectionary* readings for Morning Prayer, these daily reflections are designed to refresh and inspire times of personal prayer. The aim is to provide rich, contemporary and engaging insights into Scripture.

Each page lists the lectionary readings for the day, with the main psalms for that day highlighted in **bold**. The Collect of the day – either the *Common Worship* collect or the shorter additional collect – is also included.

For those using this book in conjunction with a service of Morning Prayer, the following conventions apply: a psalm printed in parentheses is omitted if it has been used as the opening canticle at that office; a psalm marked with an asterisk may be shortened if desired.

A short reflection is provided on either the Old or New Testament reading. Popular writers, experienced ministers, biblical scholars and theologians contribute to this series, all bringing their own emphases, enthusiasms and approaches to biblical interpretation to bear.

Regular users of Morning Prayer and *Time to Pray* (from *Common Worship: Daily Prayer*) and anyone who follows the lectionary for their regular Bible reading will benefit from the rich variety of traditions represented in these stimulating and accessible pieces.

The book also includes both a simple form of Common Worship: Morning Prayer (see pages 48–49) and a short form of Night Prayer, also known as Compline (see pages 52–55), particularly for the benefit of those readers who are new to the habit of the Daily Office or for any reader while travelling.

# Making a habit of Lent

It's often said that life is about choices. But a life based on perpetual choice would be a nightmare. To avoid the tyranny of having to make perpetual choices, we develop habits. The point about habits is to develop good ones. That's what Lent is about. Here are the six most important ones.

- **Habit number one: look inside your heart.**

  Examine yourself. Find inside yourself some things that shouldn't be there. If they're hard to extract, get some help. Name them by sitting or kneeling down with a trusted friend or pastor, and just say, 'These things shouldn't be there. Please help me let God take them away.' Self-examination isn't just about finding things that shouldn't be there. It's also about finding things that are there but have been neglected. That's sometimes where vocation begins. Look inside your heart. Do it. Make a habit of it.

- **Habit number two: pray.**

  Don't get in a pickle about whether to pray with a book or just freestyle: do both. Once a day each. Simple as that. Think about the way you shop. Sometimes I shop with a list; sometimes not. Sometimes it's a pleasure; sometimes it's a necessity; sometimes it's a pain. Sometimes I go with someone else, or even help someone else to go; sometimes I go on my own. Sometimes it's about big things; sometimes it's about little things. Sometimes I really think carefully about it, and check through a kind of recipe list; sometimes I just do it, and realize later what I've forgotten. Prayer's just as varied. Just do it. Make a habit of it.

- **Habit number three: fast.**

  Fasting is about toughening yourself up so you don't go all pathetic at the first smell or sight of something sweet or tasty. It's about making yourself someone to be reckoned with and not a pushover. Make a pattern of life so you don't just drift to the mobile phone or email or internet as a transitional object. Stand in solidarity with those who don't get to choose. If you can't give up a single meal, do you really care about global hunger? And learn how to be really hungry. Hungry for righteousness. Hungry for justice and peace. Hungry, fundamentally, for Easter – hungry for the resurrection only God can bring in Christ. Do it. Make a habit of it.

- **Habit number four: give money away.**

  'Ah,' you may say, 'I'm in a tight spot right now: I don't have any money.' Let me tell you now: there will never be a time in your life when you think it's a good time for giving money away. Try to tie your money to your prayers. Give money to something you believe in, and pray for the organisation you give money to. Just do it. Make a habit of it.

- **Habit number five: read the Bible.**

  Imagine you were going into a crowded airport to meet someone you were longing to see but weren't sure you'd recognize. And imagine you had a photo album of pictures that showed them in a thousand different activities. Wouldn't you study that photo album so you'd almost committed it to memory? That's what the Bible is – a series of portrayals of God, and we study it to get to know God better so we'll have no recognition problems in a crowd. Genesis has 50 chapters: you can almost do it in Lent. You can get through a couple of Paul's letters a week. There's a dozen minor prophets: read a couple a week. Find a nether region in the Bible, and go digging. Buy an accessible commentary and follow a few verses each day. Just do it. Make a habit of it.

- **Habit number six: repair broken relationships.**

  This is the last one and, for many people, the toughest. We've probably, many of us, got one big relationship that's all wrong – and maybe there's not a whole lot we can do about it. Maybe it's just a matter of keeping out of someone's way, if we've done them wrong, or trying to be civil, if they've hurt us. Now may not be the time to make things better. Now may not yet be God's time. But that doesn't mean we let all our other relationships get to that kind of place. Is there someone out there, a sibling, a rival, a long-time friend, a person who always felt inferior to you? Could you write that person a letter this Lent to say some things you've always appreciated about them but you've never told them? You can make it subtle. You can dress it up as something else. But could you see your way to that? And what about people whose names you don't know, people from whom you're estranged without ever having done the damage yourself? Could you make a new friend this Lent? Do it. Make a habit of it.

May you have a holy Lent, rooted and grounded in love.

*Samuel Wells*

3

# The importance of daily prayer

Daily prayer is a way of sustaining that most special of all relationships. It helps if we want to pray, but it can be sufficient to want to want to pray, or even to want to want to want to pray! The direction of the heart is what matters, not its achievements. Gradually we are shaped and changed by the practice of daily prayer. Apprentices in prayer never graduate, but we become a little bit more the people God wants us to be.

**Prayer isn't a technique; it's a relationship**, and it starts in the most ordinary, instinctive reactions to everyday life:

- **Gratitude**: good things are always happening to us, however small.
- **Wonder**: we often see amazing things in nature and in people but pass them by.
- **Need**: we bump into scores of needs every day.
- **Sorrow**: we mess up.

Prayer is taking those instincts and stretching them out before God. The rules then are: start small, stay natural, be honest.

**Here are four ways of putting some structure around daily prayer**.

1 **The Quiet Time**. This is the classic way of reading a passage of the Bible, using Bible reading reflections like those in this book, and then praying naturally about the way the passage has struck you, taking to God the questions, resolutions, hopes, fears and other responses that have arisen within you.

2 **The Daily Office**. This is a structured way of reading Scripture and psalms, and praying for individuals, the world, the day ahead, etc. It keeps us anchored in the Lectionary, the basic reading of the Church, and so ensures that we engage with the breadth of Scripture, rather than just with our favourite passages. It also puts us in living touch with countless others around the world who are doing something similar. There is a simple form of Morning Prayer on pages 48–49 of this book, and a form of Night Prayer (Compline) on pages 52–55. Fuller forms can be found in *Common Worship: Daily Prayer*.

3 **Holy Reading**. Also known as *Lectio Divina*, this is a tried and trusted way of feeding and meditating on the Bible, described more fully on pages 6–7 of this book. In essence, here is how it is done:

- *Read:* Read the passage slowly until a phrase catches your attention.
- *Reflect:* Chew the phrase carefully, drawing the goodness out of it.
- *Respond:* Pray about the thoughts and feelings that have surfaced in you.
- *Rest:* You may want to rest in silence for a while.
- *Repeat:* Carry on with the passage …

4 **Silence**. In our distracted culture some people are drawn more to silence than to words. This will involve *centring* (hunkering down), *focusing* on a short biblical phrase (e.g. 'Come, Holy Spirit'), *waiting* (repeating the phrase as necessary), and *ending* (perhaps with the Lord's Prayer). The length of time is irrelevant.

**There are, of course, as many ways of praying as there are people to pray**. There are no right or wrong ways to pray. 'Pray as you can, not as you can't', is wise advice. The most important thing is to make sure there is sufficient structure to keep prayer going when it's a struggle as well as when it's a joy. Prayer is too important to leave to chance.

*+John Pritchard*

## *Lectio Divina* – a way of reading the Bible

*Lectio Divina* is a contemplative way of reading the Bible. It dates back to the early centuries of the Christian Church and was established as a monastic practice by Benedict in the sixth century. It is a way of praying the Scriptures that leads us deeper into God's word. We slow down. We read a short passage more than once. We chew it over slowly and carefully. We savour it. Scripture begins to speak to us in a new way. It speaks to us personally, and aids that union we have with God through Christ, who is himself the Living Word.

Make sure you are sitting comfortably. Breathe slowly and deeply. Ask God to speak to you through the passage that you are about to read.

This way of praying starts with our silence. We often make the mistake of thinking prayer is about what we say to God. It is actually the other way round. God wants to speak to us. He will do this through the Scriptures. So don't worry about what to say. Don't worry if nothing jumps out at you at first. God is patient. He will wait for the opportunity to get in. He will give you a word and lead you to understand its meaning for you today.

### First reading: Listen

As you read the passage listen for a word or phrase that attracts you. Allow it to arise from the passage as if it is God's word for you today. Sit in silence repeating the word or phrase in your head.

Then say the word or phrase aloud.

### Second reading: Ponder

As you read the passage again, ask how this word or phrase speaks to your life and why it has connected with you. Ponder it carefully. Don't worry if you get distracted – it may be part of your response to offer to God. Sit in silence and then frame a single sentence that begins to say aloud what this word or phrase says to you.

### Third reading: Pray

As you read the passage for the last time, ask what Christ is calling from you. What is it that you need to do or consider or relinquish or take on as a result of what God is saying to you in this word or phrase? In the silence that follows the reading, pray for the grace of the Spirit to plant this word in your heart.

If you are in a group, talk for a few minutes and pray with each other.

If you are on your own, speak your prayer to God either aloud or in the silence of your heart.

If there is time, you may even want to read the passage a fourth time, and then end with the same silence before God with which you began.

*+Stephen Cottrell*

## Wednesday 1 March

### Ash Wednesday

Psalm **38**
Daniel 9.3-6, 17-19
1 Timothy 6.6-19

### 1 Timothy 6.6-19

*'... take hold of the life that really is life' (v.19)*

And so to Lent, the time when we go out with Jesus into the wilderness. In this deserted place, we must be content with the basic necessities of life. Money is no use where there is nothing to buy, and no one to sell it or be impressed by our wealth. Hungry, thirsty, hot and impoverished, we must learn in the desert what it is to have 'enough'. And we must learn to be content with it.

The Bible offers little comfort to the rich, who have other comforts to rely on. That is their problem. Christianity encourages us to rejoice in all the good things that the world affords, but learn to do without them. Although there are Old Testament texts that view prosperity as a sign of God's blessing, its harshest words are reserved for the rich who neglect the poor. When *we* put our riches first, as our first love, everything else is underrated – the gifts of nature, our relationships, our neighbour's needs, those who have nothing. 'Trapped by many senseless and harmful desires', our spiritual lives will soon be in ruin and our love of God destroyed.

In the wilderness we may find other temptations, but out there we stand a chance of learning to be content with what we need – rather than consuming more and more of things we don't – and thus 'to take hold of the life that really is life'.

COLLECT

Almighty and everlasting God,
you hate nothing that you have made
and forgive the sins of all those who are penitent:
create and make in us new and contrite hearts
that we, worthily lamenting our sins
and acknowledging our wretchedness,
may receive from you, the God of all mercy,
perfect remission and forgiveness;
through Jesus Christ your Son our Lord,
who is alive and reigns with you,
in the unity of the Holy Spirit,
one God, now and for ever.

*Reflection by* **Jeff Astley**

Psalms **77** *or* 90, **92**
Jeremiah 2.14-32
John 4.1-26

**Thursday 2 March**

### John 4.1-26

*'... give me this water, so that I may never be thirsty' (v.15)*

In a narrative that echoes the meeting in Genesis 24 of Abraham's servant with Rebekah, who became the bride of Isaac, Jesus requests a drink at a well from a stranger. In doing so, he breaks two taboos: speaking to a woman in a public place (cf. v.27) and associating with a Samaritan, whose mixed ancestry was thought to exclude them from the privileges of being a Jew.

The conversation will end both with the first use of the formula 'I am', which at least resonates with the great texts of God's self-revelation (such as Exodus 3.14; Isaiah 41.4,10 and 43.10-13), and with an emphasis on recognizing God's true Spirit in true worship (which is not here being restricted to 'internal' worship). First, though, John presents another of his potent metaphors that are so open to misunderstanding by the literal-minded: the image of water.

In Scripture and hymnody, the chaotic primeval floods are tamed by God's creative power into fountains, wells and streams that carry life, wisdom and salvation. Biologically, water is essential to life as we know it; psychologically – and therefore spiritually – it is a powerful natural symbol, both of cleansing and of slaking the thirst that warns of desiccation and death. Hence the sacrament of baptism, in which we are immersed in Christ, like a wilting plant bought from an incompetent nursery, to absorb God's gift of the life that will last.

Holy God,
our lives are laid open before you:
rescue us from the chaos of sin
and through the death of your Son
bring us healing and make us whole
in Jesus Christ our Lord.

COLLECT

## Friday 3 March

Psalms **3**, 7 *or* **88** (95)
Jeremiah 3.6-22
John 4.27-42

### John 4.27-42

*'Surely no one has brought him something to eat?' (v.33)*

In John's Gospel, Jesus accepts the title of Messiah first from the lips of a Samaritan woman. For her, Jesus is initially 'a Jew' and then 'a prophet', but she later becomes the catalyst of the much greater confession of Jesus as 'the Saviour of the world'.

Now, however, it is the disciples' turn to miss the point of Jesus' metaphorical theology, this time over the symbol of food. After our need for water, food is the next great necessity of life. Still operating in one dimension, the disciples fret that their master isn't eating enough. His response in verse 32 points to another, higher dimension of life and nourishment, but they are still finding it hard to raise their sights above the mundane concerns of living.

Jesus pushes the symbol further, however, by speaking of their responsibility as harvesters, reaping where others have sown. On God's timescale, the patriarchs and prophets can share the joys of this harvest, while at the very start of Jesus' ministry the fields are already ripe for the reapers, rich with the 'fruit for eternal life'.

God's food, like God's drink, is the gift that keeps on giving and will endure. It is present now and will outlast everything else that can give us life – as will the rewards due to those who gather in its harvest.

COLLECT

Almighty and everlasting God,
you hate nothing that you have made
and forgive the sins of all those who are penitent:
create and make in us new and contrite hearts
that we, worthily lamenting our sins
and acknowledging our wretchedness,
may receive from you, the God of all mercy,
perfect remission and forgiveness;
through Jesus Christ your Son our Lord,
who is alive and reigns with you,
in the unity of the Holy Spirit,
one God, now and for ever.

*Reflection by* **Jeff Astley**

Psalms **71** *or* 96, **97**, 100
Jeremiah 4.1-18
John 4.43-end

### John 4.43-end

*'... come down before my little boy dies' (v.49)*

For this Gospel's second 'sign', Jesus is back in Cana. But this is a more significant and life-giving gift, and it is offered to someone who is presumably a gentile.

The health of children was extremely precarious until relatively recently. In the first century, only about a half of all children reached the age of five. Such statistics would have done nothing to dampen a parent's despair when one of their own children fell ill. Despite his exalted status, this 'royal official' is utterly helpless in face of this impending tragedy.

Jesus' comment in verse 48 seems dismissive and cruel. There is no indication that this man is lusting after signs and wonders, or that he is to be numbered among those who do not honour their home-grown prophets (v.44 – where Jesus is conceivably speaking about Jerusalem or this world in general). The evangelists wrote their Gospels, however, for later Christians to ponder. As with the story of Thomas (John 20.24-29), we are to put ourselves in the place of someone who has faith without having witnessed incontrovertible evidence. All that Jesus requires of us is a true and honest acknowledgment of our need, and the faith that the one from whom we seek help *also* cares and that his word may be trusted. This child's healing also symbolizes therefore the new life that Jesus brings and will bring, whether we are yet worthy of it or not.

Holy God,
our lives are laid open before you:
rescue us from the chaos of sin
and through the death of your Son
bring us healing and make us whole
in Jesus Christ our Lord.

COLLECT

## Monday 6 March

Psalms 10, **11** *or* **98**, 99, 101
Jeremiah 4.19-end
John 5.1-18

### John 5.1-18
*'Do you want to be made well?' (v.6)*

This passage may lead us to wonder how to view this chronically sick man. He is not recorded as thanking Jesus, but we are told that he reports Jesus to his enemies concerning what was done that Sabbath. Jesus tells him not to sin any more, but are we to infer from this that his sickness had been caused by his sin? Elsewhere, Jesus heals the sick as he forgives – or by his forgiving – their sins (cf. Mark 2.5), but he also sometimes seems to dissociate suffering and sin (cf. John 9.2-3).

The word translated 'well' or 'healthy' is used many times in this passage. It reminds us that the vocabulary of salvation and that of healing, or being made whole, are closely related. Unquestionably they are analogous concepts. Jesus' closeness to his Father means that he will always do the Father's remedial work whenever it is needed, whether this involves spiritual or physical repair. Or both.

But what was *Jesus'* 'sin'? The commentators disagree: his offence may have been healing on the Sabbath, or getting the healed man to engage in the work of carrying his bed away. For John, it was mainly that Jesus made himself 'equal to God' by his words, but surely also by his deeds. We, too, may get annoyed when someone's generosity shows up the narrowness of our own compassion. But what if God uncovers the restrictions of our theology?

COLLECT

Almighty God,
whose Son Jesus Christ fasted forty days in the wilderness,
and was tempted as we are, yet without sin:
give us grace to discipline ourselves in obedience to your Spirit;
and, as you know our weakness,
so may we know your power to save;
through Jesus Christ your Son our Lord,
who is alive and reigns with you,
in the unity of the Holy Spirit,
one God, now and for ever.

*Reflection by* **Jeff Astley**

Psalm **44** *or* **106**\* (*or* 103)
Jeremiah 5.1-19
John 5.19-29

## John 5.19-29

*'... what he sees the Father doing' (v.19)*

God's coming reign and the resurrection of the last days, both of which the pious hoped for, are 'now here' in Jesus, the Son. In other Gospels, this new thing is entitled the kingdom of God or of 'heaven'. In John it is called 'eternal life'. Whatever its name, it begins *now* and it demands a decision, from those who now face Jesus, as to whether or not he is recognizable as the son of this father.

This thing is not yet complete, though. It has still to come 'with power' (cf. Mark 9.1) in the final 'resurrection of life' (John 5.29). But in a way the judgement has already been made by how people respond to the Son. For if they do not honour Jesus, how will they ever honour his father – or hear his voice (vv. 22-23, 28)?

It is of the first importance that we learn to see what God is doing, and learn to see it *as* God's work. Even the Son has to learn, like an apprentice, 'whatever the Father does'. Having learned in this way, we shall see that healing and removing sick beds are just the sort of thing that God would do: for that is the sort of God that God is.

To see that is to see the kingdom, and the life that lasts. It is to see God at work, down by Sheep Gate Pool.

Heavenly Father,
your Son battled with the powers of darkness,
and grew closer to you in the desert:
help us to use these days to grow in wisdom and prayer
that we may witness to your saving love
in Jesus Christ our Lord.

COLLECT

Psalms **6**, 17 *or* 110, **111**, 112
Jeremiah 5.20-end
John 5.30-end

### John 5.30-end

*'... seek the glory that comes from the one who alone is God' (v.44)*

Who is in the dock here? Jesus calls his witnesses for the defence: himself (but this, regrettably, is inadmissible in the Law), John the Baptist (who is described as the lamp lit from the light), Jesus' own works and the Father. An impressive line-up.

But the author knows that it is Jesus' enemies who are really on trial. They have ignored all the evidence, even the testimony of God. They have pored over the Scriptures but entirely missed the point of them, neither hearing God's voice through them nor allowing God's word to live within themselves.

The problem here is the problem of the source of glory. Seeking and accepting it 'from human beings', 'from one another', has blinded them to the true light that can only come from God – from the one whose glory transcends everything that the world has to offer.

Perhaps it does all begin, as it must end, with love. Unless we want God, unless we have love *for* God, we will never want the Son or acclaim his works as the works of a loving father. Love comes first, before worship and before belief. If we want a God we can 'believe in' – a God whom we can love and praise – we must first believe in love. For 'whatever your heart clings to and confides in, that is really your God' (Martin Luther). And we can only worship the true God.

COLLECT

Almighty God,
whose Son Jesus Christ fasted forty days in the wilderness,
and was tempted as we are, yet without sin:
give us grace to discipline ourselves in obedience to your Spirit;
and, as you know our weakness,
so may we know your power to save;
through Jesus Christ your Son our Lord,
who is alive and reigns with you,
in the unity of the Holy Spirit,
one God, now and for ever.

*Reflection by* **Jeff Astley**

Psalms **42**, 43 *or* 113, **115**
Jeremiah 6.9-21
John 6.1-15

### John 6.1-15

*'But what are they among so many people?' (v.9)*

Every Gospel has made room for this story; we may wonder why. Its echoes of the Eucharist, or at least of the Last Supper, are stronger in the other Gospel versions than they are in John. He omits some of their details, but he alone mentions the human source of the feast, which is small in every way (v.9). And only he reports Jesus' concern that none of the leftovers are wasted (v.12). In Greek the verb is 'lost' and it is used, significantly, at verse 39, but it can also be translated 'perishes' (at verse 27 – again significantly).

There is a touching tenderness here: a practical concern for the hungry and their nagging, physical needs, as well as a symbolic concern for the little things of life and the world's broken fragments. The Church doesn't always share Jesus' concerns for such 'little ones' (cf. Mark 9.42; Luke 12.32). It especially needs to ponder on its Lord's ability to create great abundance out of small and inadequate materials.

In the second-century document, *The Didache*, the text 'concerning the Eucharist' includes this prayer: 'Even as this broken bread was scattered over the hills, and was gathered together and became one, so let your Church be gathered together from the ends of the earth into your kingdom.' This is to happen to 'the glory and the power' of God 'through Jesus Christ for ever'. May it be so.

Heavenly Father,
your Son battled with the powers of darkness,
and grew closer to you in the desert:
help us to use these days to grow in wisdom and prayer
that we may witness to your saving love
in Jesus Christ our Lord.

COLLECT

*Reflection by* **Jeff Astley**     15

**Friday 10 March**

Psalm **22** *or* **139**
Jeremiah 6.22-end
John 6.16-27

### John 6.16-27

*'It is I; do not be afraid' (v.20)*

In their accounts of Jesus walking on the water, both Mark and Matthew report the wind ceasing when he enters the disciples' boat; in all three Gospels other than John there is a further, separate account of the stilling of a storm. In John, however, the 'strong wind' is not said to die down, although the boat 'immediately ... reached the land towards which they were going'. In all these stories the disciples' fear is palpable, but here it seems to arise less from the storm than from other factors: perhaps the dark and the general eeriness of the scene, but also the sense of the awe-ful majesty of the power of God, glimpsed striding over the waves.

There are plenty of warnings in this Gospel about taking things too literally, too much 'at face value', and thereby missing the divine depth of the signs that God provides. Verses 26-27 caution us against making this mistake over the loaves and the feeding of the multitude. Other miracles of Jesus may be open to similar misreadings. John doesn't expect his text to feed a pious expectation that Jesus will walk on water to rescue us from our inadequate vessels and feeble maritime skills. There is a greater salvation that we need from him, and a greater miracle. For what other hope do we have of journeying to a secure mooring and entering God's safe harbour?

COLLECT

Almighty God,
whose Son Jesus Christ fasted forty days in the wilderness,
and was tempted as we are, yet without sin:
give us grace to discipline ourselves in obedience to your Spirit;
and, as you know our weakness,
so may we know your power to save;
through Jesus Christ your Son our Lord,
who is alive and reigns with you,
in the unity of the Holy Spirit,
one God, now and for ever.

*Reflection by* **Jeff Astley**

## John 6.27-40
*'I am the bread of life' (v.35)*

In the words of biblical scholar John Marsh, Jesus 'is the gift he brings'. 'The bread of life' is the bread that is the source of life, and also the 'living bread'. It nourishes us, fills us, satisfies us, enlivens us. The symbolism chimes with the Church's eucharistic practice, in which the body of Christ is ingested and becomes part of us, part of our life.

In the period between the Old and New Testaments, 'the manna in the wilderness' was interpreted as God's wisdom, which was itself the word of life and the fulfilment of the Law. In taking to himself the divine word of revelation, 'I am', Jesus presents himself as this work of God's self-disclosure.

The bread is what God *does*: a gift that feeds the hungry, one that requires nothing of them but their acceptance that it is food and that it will indeed fill them. All we have to do – the only 'spiritual labour which makes it possible' to earn this food (as Anglican Franciscan scholar Barnabas Lindars put it) – is to accept and trust Jesus. John and Paul are at one in this.

To have this bread is to have life, life that is never going to be lost. The bread that 'comes down from heaven and gives life to the world' will not be lost, nor will any whom the Son has been given. Why? Because this filling up and making full, this *fulfilment*, is what God intends – and will ensure.

Heavenly Father,
your Son battled with the powers of darkness,
and grew closer to you in the desert:
help us to use these days to grow in wisdom and prayer
that we may witness to your saving love
in Jesus Christ our Lord.

COLLECT

**Monday 13 March**

Psalms 26, **32** or 123, 124, 125, **126**
Jeremiah 7.21-end
John 6.41-51

### John 6.41-51

*'Is not this Jesus, the son of Joseph ...?' (v.42)*

To be known by our association to others – 'so you're Wendy's sister/George's wife/Peter's colleague/Sarah's friend ...' – can be both a blessing and a curse. Even with regard to the best of relationships, to be defined by our connection to others can feel belittling. We feel this not only when it means we are dismissed, but also if it seems as if it's the reason we are honoured.

Jesus was being discounted because of his family ties. Although we are told that he honoured Mary and Joseph, we also know that his identity, though shaped by them, was not determined by them. It was his identity as the son of his heavenly Father that provided his security: 'the one who is from God; he has seen the Father'.

Letting go of our labels may be a relief or it may be a threat. However we feel about our personal relationships, we too are offered a new identity in Christ as joint heirs of the kingdom and recipients of the promise of eternal life. Our identity in Christ is a gift from God, and frees us to become who God desires us to be, not what others expect us to be.

Our new identity offers security but is a challenge as well as a comfort. The bread of life, broken for us, is given for the life of the whole world. Like those first disciples, we too are required to share what we have been given.

COLLECT

Almighty God,
you show to those who are in error the light of your truth,
that they may return to the way of righteousness:
grant to all those who are admitted
    into the fellowship of Christ's religion,
that they may reject those things
    that are contrary to their profession,
and follow all such things as are agreeable to the same;
through our Lord Jesus Christ,
who is alive and reigns with you,
in the unity of the Holy Spirit,
one God, now and for ever.

*Reflection by* **Libby Lane**

Psalms **50** *or* **132**, 133
Jeremiah 8.1-15
John 6.52-59

**Tuesday 14 March**

### John 6.52-59

*'... my flesh is true food' (v.55)*

Nourishment is about calories and hydration, balance of proteins and carbohydrates, minerals and vitamins – necessary for our physical and mental wellbeing. But, for those of us blessed with plenty and choice, being well fed is not only about sustenance but is also one of life's pleasures. It is about taste and texture, aroma and visual stimulus. It is sensual as well as practical, often about experience as well as function.

'Taste and see that the Lord is good' the psalmist encourages us (Psalm 34.8). That sounds as though being nourished by God gives pleasure as well as sustenance.

Jesus says that he is our true food. The word made flesh, broken for us, is the source of real food that nourishes, sustains and delights us. What are the ways that we can 'feed' on him? If Jesus is our true food, perhaps there are other things that falsely claim to feed us. So, what else might we be relying on for that which Jesus best supplies?

It is not, necessarily, that other things that feed our sense of wellbeing are not good in themselves. But how do we avoid inappropriately relying on them instead of Jesus? Or allowing them to detract from Jesus rather than glorify him? How, instead, might we recognize and acknowledge Christ in life's pleasures, and in the people and things that give us support and help us to flourish?

Almighty God,
by the prayer and discipline of Lent
may we enter into the mystery of Christ's sufferings,
and by following in his Way
come to share in his glory;
through Jesus Christ our Lord.

COLLECT

*Reflection by* **Libby Lane**    19

## Wednesday 15 March

Psalm **35** *or* 119.153-end
Jeremiah 8.18 – 9.11
John 6.60-end

### John 6.60-end

*'You have the words of eternal life' (v.68)*

The author of the *Father Brown* stories, G. K. Chesterton, wrote: 'The Christian ideal has not been tried and found wanting. It has been found difficult; and left untried.' Jesus' listeners found much of what he said difficult, it seems. Jesus' words were not simply dismissed by those who were opposed to him. Those who were closest to him also struggled with what he was saying. There is a lot that we might find difficult about Jesus' teaching today too. Perhaps we find it too complex: what does he mean? Maybe we consider it too troublesome: what does he expect? For some it may seem too offensive: who does he think he is? It is demanding, difficult. Is it therefore too much?

'The Christian ideal', as Chesterton puts it, does stretch us in every way. Following Jesus makes demands on the ways we think, the ways we act, the ways we feel. However, it offers a great deal more than it demands. Jesus, Simon Peter recognized, has the words of eternal life. Indeed, the writer of the Gospel of John would have us realize, Jesus *is* the Word of Life.

Perhaps it's only possible to follow the demands that we hear through the words of Jesus if we hear them as those in a relationship with the one who speaks them. Perhaps this teaching is too difficult (v.60) unless, through Jesus' love for us and in us, his words become 'spirit and life' (v.63).

COLLECT

Almighty God,
you show to those who are in error the light of your truth,
that they may return to the way of righteousness:
grant to all those who are admitted
    into the fellowship of Christ's religion,
that they may reject those things
    that are contrary to their profession,
and follow all such things as are agreeable to the same;
through our Lord Jesus Christ,
who is alive and reigns with you,
in the unity of the Holy Spirit,
one God, now and for ever.

Psalms **34** or **143**, 146
Jeremiah 9.12-24
John 7.1-13

### John 7.1-13

*'For not even his brothers believed in him' (v.5)*

The Gospels tell us that Jesus' relationship with his own family was complicated. It appears that his brothers had confidence in what he was doing. It seems that they wanted him to be known and followed more widely. Yet, Jesus turned them down, and the Gospel writer comments that they did not believe in him.

So, Jesus' brothers' desire for his ministry to be more widely recognized was not yet belief. Perhaps they liked the attention and acclamation that came from being associated with someone well known and successful. That was not Jesus' purpose though.

It can be frustrating and disheartening to discover the things we have suggested or worked at for Jesus and the Church being rejected or overlooked. We can feel angry if those same things are then taken up by others at a later time. We can feel belittled when approval is given to someone else for a contribution when it seems it was withheld from us. Letting go of our own agendas and priorities requires the kind of patience and humility that may only be possible when received as gifts of the Spirit.

Jesus' brothers wanted the right things but at the wrong time and by the world's means. His brothers had not yet learnt to trust Jesus' judgement and to do thing his way rather than the world's way. That can be one of the hardest lessons to learn.

Almighty God,
by the prayer and discipline of Lent
may we enter into the mystery of Christ's sufferings,
and by following in his Way
come to share in his glory;
through Jesus Christ our Lord.

COLLECT

## Friday 17 March

Psalms 40, **41** *or* 142, **144**
Jeremiah 10.1-16
John 7.14-24

### John 7.14-24

*'... and there is nothing false in him' (v.18)*

The word 'sincere' is from the Latin, '*sin*' and '*cere*', meaning, literally, 'without wax'. The phrase came to be used to signify that someone was exactly as they seemed, without pretence. It arose because Roman sculptors would use flawed marble, or make mistakes in carving, and then mask the imperfections with wax, so that what they presented seemed to be perfect when it was not. These flaws might become apparent only after a long time but eventually they would show up. The wax would react differently from the marble to extremes of weather, or to wear and tear, or would become discoloured, or would degrade and crumble.

To attribute sincerity to someone, therefore, is a big claim. It does mean that 'there is nothing false in him'. We all have things to hide. We exaggerate or minimize aspects of ourselves. We are economical with what we choose to reveal. We are sometimes blind to our own faults. Eventually, over time, though those flaws become apparent, not only to others but, if we are prepared to see them, to ourselves. Such self-knowledge is a necessary aspect of maturity. Facing up to our imperfections is a precursor to trying to address them. In the end, none of us can be entirely '*sin cere*', and we will need to repent both our failings and our desire to hide them. Jesus, though, had 'nothing false in him', and so we look to him for a model of sincere living, the forgiveness of our own insincerity and the grace to be as we truly are without shame or pride.

COLLECT

Almighty God,
you show to those who are in error the light of your truth,
that they may return to the way of righteousness:
grant to all those who are admitted
    into the fellowship of Christ's religion,
that they may reject those things
    that are contrary to their profession,
and follow all such things as are agreeable to the same;
through our Lord Jesus Christ,
who is alive and reigns with you,
in the unity of the Holy Spirit,
one God, now and for ever.

*Reflection by* **Libby Lane**

Psalms 3, **25** *or* **147**
Jeremiah 10.17-24
John 7.25-36

### John 7.25-36

*'Can it be that ... this is the Messiah?' (v.26)*

The prophet Jeremiah speaks of God's encouragement: 'When you search for me, you will find me; if you seek me with all your heart' (Jeremiah 29.13). The people were longing for God's Messiah to come, but when Jesus came, many were confused and uncertain; they did not recognize or acknowledge him as the one they had been searching for.

That Jesus did not meet expectations says more perhaps about the expectations than it does about Jesus. When we long for God, do we blind ourselves to recognizing Jesus because our expectations are flawed or limited?

Jesus was consistent and authentic. He was clear about who he was and what he was called to do. Again and again he articulated in word and deed the truth about himself. Jesus spoke with authority. This was not because he came from the right place or had studied with the right people but because he spoke only the words given by his heavenly Father. Jesus acted with authority. His signs pointed to the One who had sent him. Jesus said and showed that he is the Messiah, the one from God.

'I am ... I am ... I am', Jesus repeats five times just in these few verses. In Jesus Christ, the Messiah, promised of God, God himself, Yahweh, the great 'I am', is with us. God, it seems, fulfils the promise to be with us, but in unexpected ways.

Almighty God,
by the prayer and discipline of Lent
may we enter into the mystery of Christ's sufferings,
and by following in his Way
come to share in his glory;
through Jesus Christ our Lord.

COLLECT

## Monday 20 March
### Joseph of Nazareth

### Matthew 13.54–end
*'Is not this the carpenter's son?' (v.55)*

The people of Nazareth took offence at Jesus. They resented his ministry and questioned his wisdom and power. They cast doubt on his authority to teach. 'Is not this the carpenter's son?'

They meant the question disparagingly, but why would Jesus be ashamed to be known as Joseph's son? Matthew, earlier in his Gospel, identifies Joseph as 'a righteous man' (Matthew 1.19). Joseph's treatment of Mary reveals him to be generous and gentle. His response to the message of the angel about Jesus' conception shows him to be open-minded as well as open-hearted. His response to the message of the angel about Herod's intentions shows him to be decisive and determined. Joseph was faithful, loving, courageous and godly. It was no disgrace to be known as the carpenter's son.

Sometimes the things that other people would disparage or look down on in us are the very things of which we should be proud. They may be the things that God has used to bring us to maturity and godliness. God chose Joseph to be father to his son, and he was faithful to that calling. Jesus had much to be grateful for because of Joseph.

Perhaps the example of Joseph can encourage us to be thankful to God for those things that have been influential in our lives but get overlooked or undervalued. Perhaps the example of Joseph can encourage us to do as God asks of us without expectation of recognition or reward.

COLLECT

God our Father,
who from the family of your servant David
raised up Joseph the carpenter
to be the guardian of your incarnate Son
and husband of the Blessed Virgin Mary:
give us grace to follow him
in faithful obedience to your commands;
through Jesus Christ your Son our Lord,
who is alive and reigns with you,
in the unity of the Holy Spirit,
one God, now and for ever.

*Reflection by* **Libby Lane**

*Lent*

Psalms 6, **9** *or* **5**, 6 (8)
Jeremiah 11.18 – 12.6
John 7.53 – 8.11

**Tuesday 21 March**

### John 7.53 – 8.11
*'Has no one condemned you?' (8.10)*

There is a terrible disregard for this woman caught in adultery. There is no indication that she has been falsely accused but that seems incidental. This is about catching Jesus out, and she is collateral damage in that bigger fight. She is, to the scribes and Pharisees, it seems, a pawn easily sacrificed in a larger game plan.

Jesus is forced to face the dilemma we so often face too: how to remain clear on points of principle without losing sight of the individuals who live with the consequences. Jesus does not answer the question put to him on the point of principle. He cuts through the posturing and self-righteousness with a response that places the responsibility for the outworking of the dilemma back with those who raised it.

The scribes and Pharisees had separated themselves from the woman but Jesus reunited them with her. They had isolated her by the sin they had caught her in. Jesus' response required them to realize they stood with her. Not one of them could cast a stone because no one of them was without sin.

So often we judge ourselves against others; sometimes counting ourselves better, sometimes diminishing ourselves in comparison. This, though, is to miss the point. This story reminds us that 'all have sinned and fall short of the glory of God' (Romans 3.23). Jesus is without sin, but he chose mercy for this woman and offers mercy to us.

Almighty God,
whose most dear Son went not up to joy but first he suffered pain,
and entered not into glory before he was crucified:
mercifully grant that we, walking in the way of the cross,
may find it none other than the way of life and peace;
through Jesus Christ your Son our Lord,
who is alive and reigns with you,
in the unity of the Holy Spirit,
one God, now and for ever.

COLLECT

*Reflection by* **Libby Lane**     25

## **Wednesday 22 March**

Psalm **38** *or* **119.1-32**
Jeremiah 13.1-11
John 8.12-30

### John 8.12-30

*'... where I have come from and where I am going' (v.14)*

Jesus offers himself as light for our journey, as a route through life to follow. The path he offers is the one he walked. He says we can trust him because he knows the way. There is a wonderful simplicity in Jesus' self-assurance. Jesus is at peace because he *knows* – he knows his beginning and his end. He therefore knows the path to take.

Jesus' confidence comes from knowing his heavenly Father. The anointing of the Spirit, and time in his Father's company, set the direction of travel for Jesus. His route was determined by listening for God's voice and moving towards it. Doing what is pleasing to God was Jesus' compass.

When we come to know Jesus as the one sent from God, we have a new beginning and a new end. Our journey begins when we are forgiven and made new in Christ, and our destination is with him in glory for eternity. What comes between follows Jesus' trajectory. Our compass also points us to doing what is pleasing to God.

We walk the path Jesus trod by his light. We share his direction of travel. We too discern the way by remaining close to our heavenly Father, being open to the Spirit, spending time in prayer. The journey is not a predetermined one, but an adventure in Jesus' company.

COLLECT

Almighty God,
whose most dear Son went not up to joy but first he suffered pain,
and entered not into glory before he was crucified:
mercifully grant that we, walking in the way of the cross,
may find it none other than the way of life and peace;
through Jesus Christ your Son our Lord,
who is alive and reigns with you,
in the unity of the Holy Spirit,
one God, now and for ever.

*Reflection by* **Libby Lane**

**Thursday 23 March**

### John 8.31-47

*'If God were your Father ...' (v.42)*

When my son was about three years old, he saw a photograph of his Dad at the same age. Our son looked so like the boy in the photograph, he could not be persuaded that it was not him. There was a very strong family resemblance. Family resemblance, though, is not always physical. I have friends with adopted children about whom strangers also comment: 'Isn't he just like his dad?' In fact, they do not look alike, but the children have picked up mannerisms and character traits from their parents.

Jesus' teaching is both very hard and, simultaneously, extraordinarily generous. How terrible to hear from Jesus, 'you are not from God' (v.47). He is saying that family resemblance that is not rooted in a living relationship is as good as dead. For the Jews to say, 'Abraham is our father' (v.39) was not sufficient if they were not manifesting family characteristics. This is a hard truth for us too.

The extraordinary promise, though, is that all those who love Jesus hear his words as from God and follow his example – pick up his family traits – are members of God's household as dearly beloved children. The challenge to us, whether we trace our connection to God through generations or have newly discovered God in Christ, is to be known as God's children not because of our history but because of our living present, following Jesus so closely that others recognize God in us too.

COLLECT

Eternal God,
give us insight
to discern your will for us,
to give up what harms us,
and to seek the perfection we are promised
in Jesus Christ our Lord.

## Friday 24 March

### John 8.48-end

*'... before Abraham was, I am' (v.58)*

Jesus speaks unambiguously an outrageous truth. He doesn't hide it in a story or wrap it up in a parable. 'Very truly, I tell you' (v.58), he says. 'Listen up, this is something important, I want you to get this clear', he means. He claims identity with God, the living one, the beginning and the end. That is outrageous. He is saying, 'I am God'.

It has been reflected that our response to such a claim can only fall into one of three categories: Jesus was mad – he believes what he is saying but he is deluded; Jesus was bad – he knew what he saying was untrue, but he was a charlatan; or what Jesus says about himself is true – Jesus is indeed God made man. This lies at the heart of our faith. Who is Jesus?

Jesus says he has no choice but to speak this truth about himself. To deny it would be to deny the One who sent him. To so speak of himself therefore is not self-aggrandisement but glorifying God. If we accept this truth, there's not a lot of choice for us either. Some say Jesus is a great teacher. Some say he was a good man. Others say that he was holy, a great community leader, a prophet. That all may be true, but it is not what Jesus says of himself. If Jesus is God, I suggest, we can but rejoice, repent and be renewed.

COLLECT

Almighty God,
whose most dear Son went not up to joy but first he suffered pain,
and entered not into glory before he was crucified:
mercifully grant that we, walking in the way of the cross,
may find it none other than the way of life and peace;
through Jesus Christ your Son our Lord,
who is alive and reigns with you,
in the unity of the Holy Spirit,
one God, now and for ever.

Psalms 111, 113
1 Samuel 2.1-10
Romans 5.12-end

## Annunciation of Our Lord to the Blessed Virgin Mary

### Romans 5.12-end

*'... abundance of grace and the free gift of righteousness' (v.17)*

We are a mass of contradictions. We like a bargain or a special offer. Our consumerism is fed by sales and BOGOF ('Buy one get one free'), but we are resistant to the idea of something for nothing. We like to treat ourselves and respond to advertising that suggests 'we are worth it', but we are suspicious of extravagance.

We place value on reward for hard work. Children are disciplined in homework from an early age. Expectations of long hours at work are common. Many suffer the physical and mental health consequences of stress.

Often our public policy and political rhetoric is shaped around the idea that people get what they deserve. If good behaviour and hard work bring reward, then those who are without must be bad and lazy.

Does this make it difficult for us to accept the abundant grace and free gift of God in Christ? This may be because we first have to accept that we deserve condemnation, that we are rightly judged. We then have to recognize that we cannot earn our way into righteousness and grace. Finally, we are asked to accept God's free gift, a gift offered to all. What God offers is beyond what is reasonable or sensible. It is more than we could hope for or imagine.

In every way our salvation is countercultural. It is all the more precious for that.

We beseech you, O Lord,
pour your grace into our hearts,
that as we have known the incarnation of your Son Jesus Christ
by the message of an angel,
so by his cross and passion
we may be brought to the glory of his resurrection;
through Jesus Christ your Son our Lord,
who is alive and reigns with you,
in the unity of the Holy Spirit,
one God, now and for ever.

COLLECT

## Monday 27 March

Psalms 70, **77** *or* 27, **30**
Jeremiah 17.5-18
John 9.18-end

### John 9.18-end

*'... though I was blind, now I see' (v.25)*

After the event, the questions come: 'What did he do to you? How did he open your eyes?' (v.26) The onlookers' opinions vary, but all seem to agree that something has happened, and understanding the details of who, how and why becomes important. We read this narrative as if watching players on a stage: our vision moves from one side to the other, as we follow the range of characters portrayed.

A man is at the centre, and we see him as he takes in the world with new sight. The miracle has taken place, but Jesus' opponents suspect fraud. The man's parents verify what has happened, but are unable to explain it, or rather, they fear to do so because that would risk exclusion from the synagogue (v.22).

Yet this story is about more than an unfolding and fast-paced drama on the stage; it is also an invitation to consider the different ways in which our vision is impaired by perspectives that are life-*limiting* rather than life-*giving*. John builds this narrative layer upon layer suggesting different degrees of blindness, while at the same time enabling the one who is given sight to counter cynicism with wit, courage and humour. We should be rightly challenged by this gradual revelation and the sharp insight of the man who sees Jesus for who he really is within a context of doubt and fear. Complacency holds us back, but we are called to illuminate darkness and wilderness with hope.

COLLECT

Merciful Lord,
absolve your people from their offences,
that through your bountiful goodness
we may all be delivered from the chains of those sins
which by our frailty we have committed;
grant this, heavenly Father,
for Jesus Christ's sake, our blessed Lord and Saviour,
who is alive and reigns with you,
in the unity of the Holy Spirit,
one God, now and for ever.

*Reflection by* **Helen-Ann Hartley**

Psalms 54, **79** or 32, **36**
Jeremiah 18.1-12
John 10.1-10

## John 10.1-10

*'... I came that they may have life, and have it abundantly' (v.10)*

One of my favourite Greek words is the word for sheep: *'probaton'* or rather, *'probaaaton'* as I like to say it! The picture of sheep probing about in search of pasture and safety is at the heart of this section describing Jesus both as the door or gate and the good shepherd. There are two short parables in these verses. The first, in verses 1-2, concerns the fake shepherd who is identified as a thief because he climbs into the sheepfold rather than using the correct entrance.

The second, in verses 3-6, reveals the importance of the voice of the shepherd, which the sheep can uniquely recognize and know. Jesus is the gate or the door because he protects the sheep and enables them to seek food and thus to have life. Kenneth Bailey, who taught New Testament in Middle Eastern contexts for much of his career, describes how this scene reflects the day to-day life of Jesus' context. Sheltering for the night while in the process of seeking pasture, the sheep rest in a cave with the shepherd sleeping across its entrance. Putting himself in a vulnerable place on behalf of the sheep, the shepherd gives up his own safety to enable the sheep to rest. Jesus' designation of himself in this way places a focus on the sacrificial nature of his ministry.

In the morning, the shepherd awakes, and the sheep emerge into light receiving sustenance in pastures new.

Merciful Lord,
you know our struggle to serve you:
when sin spoils our lives
and overshadows our hearts,
come to our aid
and turn us back to you again;
through Jesus Christ our Lord.

COLLECT

**Wednesday 29 March**

Psalms 63, **90** or **34**
Jeremiah 18.13-end
John 10.11-21

### John 10.11-21

*'I am the good shepherd. The good shepherd lays down his life for the sheep' (v.11)*

We often think about the word 'good' in moral terms. In this context however, the Greek work used for 'good' means beautiful or noble. Immediately, we are drawn into a puzzling even shocking picture: how can a shepherd who gives his life for his sheep be beautiful? We shouldn't be altogether surprised at this description, since the gospel so often presents us with something unexpected rather than predictable. Still, the image jars; it seems to be over the top.

But let's think about this from another perspective. Someone does a deed for you that is self-giving and motivated not by their own desire for gain but because of their love for you. How do you respond? Over many years, I have experienced the act of foot-washing on Maundy Thursday, both the washing and the being washed. The word that immediately comes into my mind as I picture the tapestry of visual memories in my mind is 'beauty'. There is nothing to be gained, so it would seem, by such an act, yet it is not a meaningless gesture, rather an outpouring of love.

In this way, Jesus as the good shepherd is the one who is willing to pay the ultimate price for love. Through death, however, new life emerges. Beyond the risk and pain, there is resurrection and the opportunity to hope once more.

COLLECT

Merciful Lord,
absolve your people from their offences,
that through your bountiful goodness
we may all be delivered from the chains of those sins
which by our frailty we have committed;
grant this, heavenly Father,
for Jesus Christ's sake, our blessed Lord and Saviour,
who is alive and reigns with you,
in the unity of the Holy Spirit,
one God, now and for ever.

*Reflection by* **Helen-Ann Hartley**

### John 10.22-end

*'How long will you keep us in suspense? If you are the Messiah,
tell us plainly' (v.24)*

John's Gospel is thick with irony, and this passage is no exception. Isn't it obvious that Jesus is the Messiah, we might say to ourselves? The point is made persistently: many people failed to recognize Jesus, and even when it must have been impossible not to see it, this failure intensified. This, in turn, led to persecution and death, suggested here by the threat of stoning on the grounds of apparent blasphemy.

John leads us deeper into the mystery of Jesus' divine identity by increasing the risk, a sure indication that the path of following Jesus is not easy. Risk here doesn't only mean threat of death, though that is certainly possible (and worryingly probable in some places); risk also implies that we might lose heart because following Jesus becomes too hard. Risk also invites us to participate in God's mission because God and Jesus 'are one' (v.30).

The dynamic incarnational wisdom at the heart of this Gospel remains the mystery that unfolds as the narrative winds its way towards the cross and resurrection. Thus it is through engagement in God's mission that we come to know and understand more fully who Jesus is – and so often it is far from plain sailing! Jesus' opponents struggle to admit Jesus' identity, or even comprehend it. It is only through involvement that we can begin to recognize the fullness of life that is offered to us.

Merciful Lord,
you know our struggle to serve you:
when sin spoils our lives
and overshadows our hearts,
come to our aid
and turn us back to you again;
through Jesus Christ our Lord.

COLLECT

*Reflection by* **Helen-Ann Hartley**   33

## Friday 31 March

Psalm **102** *or* **31**
Jeremiah 19.14 – 20.6
John 11.1-16

### John 11.1-16

*'Lazarus is dead' (v.14)*

A statement of fact is the prelude to the last of the signs in John's Gospel. The whole point of this narrative is its emphasis on the apparent finality of death. Lazarus is most definitely dead. Jesus had known about his illness but had delayed going to see him. While it may appear harsh, the point here is similar to Jesus' rejection of his mother during the playing-out of the first of the signs in John's Gospel at Cana. Jesus is here to do the will of God, not to answer to what people want or expect of him. God's timing and purposes are not ours to control or even understand.

This is very difficult to grasp; it speaks into our tendency to present shopping lists to God in prayer. If something is broken, we want it to be fixed; if someone is ill, we want them to get better; if someone dies, we often want it not to be so, or not in that way.

We know what happens to Jesus, and therefore it is impossible to read this passage without an awareness of what happens next. Jesus' own revelation of self is elicited through his intimate interactions with the joy and pain of life. Yet as we stand with the sceptical Thomas, who pessimistically speaks of death, the irony is that we already know that Jesus will die, only we don't realize the true import of those words yet.

COLLECT

Merciful Lord,
absolve your people from their offences,
that through your bountiful goodness
we may all be delivered from the chains of those sins
which by our frailty we have committed;
grant this, heavenly Father,
for Jesus Christ's sake, our blessed Lord and Saviour,
who is alive and reigns with you,
in the unity of the Holy Spirit,
one God, now and for ever.

*Reflection by* **Helen-Ann Hartley**

### John 11.17-27

*'Yes, Lord, I believe that you are the Messiah, the Son of God,
the one coming into the world' (v.27)*

Martha's confession of faith is a bold assertion of Jesus' revealed identity in this miracle. As such it represents something of a turn-around – or perhaps at least a journey towards recognition of Jesus' identity in the midst of a very human story. Martha believes in resurrection, but here she is brought to see it revealed in Jesus. That, in turn, has an implication not only for her brother Lazarus, but also for her own faith. This is a remarkable insight.

I can think of many times when I have been confident about one thing only to have it completely turned on its head by someone else's perspective, or by an event that has taken place that makes it impossible to see something the same way again. Martha thinks Jesus is talking about the resurrection at the end of time, but Jesus is talking about the possibilities in the here and now.

We can think about the possible emotional maturity that Martha experiences as she comes to such an assertion of who Jesus is. Or perhaps she says the words, and then wonders where such insight came from? Perhaps she spends the rest of her life working out just what it all means? We cannot know, but we can surely marvel at the boldness of this statement of faith, and make it our own too.

Merciful Lord,
you know our struggle to serve you:
when sin spoils our lives
and overshadows our hearts,
come to our aid
and turn us back to you again;
through Jesus Christ our Lord.

COLLECT

*Reflection by* **Helen-Ann Hartley**     35

**Monday 3 April**

Psalms **73**, 121 *or* **44**
Jeremiah 21.1-10
John 11.28-44

### John 11.28-44

*'Jesus began to weep' (v.35)*

This verse, light in words, is heavy with emotion. Every detail matters in the Gospel, and in the midst of the profound insight into Jesus' divine identity, we are reminded that Jesus is human. Not only does he weep here, but both before and after this, he is also angry. The Greek evokes the image of a horse snorting loudly, so not only do we see emotion, but we hear it and see its effects too. One of the challenges of the biblical narrative is that we relate to it primarily through words on a page. Our literary minds are trained to read, but not all people or cultures prioritize such interactions.

An indication of this is the opportunity we have to listen to something that is being read, but then we are dependent upon a reader doing that well. The Gospel starts as an oral tradition, but before even that, as a series of life experiences. Jesus' weeping is caused by the obvious distress of those around him, but also by Jesus' own grief at the death of a friend.

Jesus knows that God is purposing Lazarus' death to God's glory. Jesus is bound up in that too, yet it is the shocking irony that, in order to experience triumph through Lazarus' own resurrection, Jesus must first walk through the shadow of grief and despair. So Jesus weeps, as we wait to see what happens next.

COLLECT

Most merciful God,
who by the death and resurrection of your Son Jesus Christ
delivered and saved the world:
grant that by faith in him who suffered on the cross
we may triumph in the power of his victory;
through Jesus Christ your Son our Lord,
who is alive and reigns with you,
in the unity of the Holy Spirit,
one God, now and for ever.

*Reflection by* **Helen-Ann Hartley**

### John 11.45-end

*'... better ... to have one man die ... than to have the whole nation destroyed' (v.50)*

With today's Lectionary reading, we enter a more focused part of our journey towards Holy Week: Passiontide. Lazarus' resurrection garners a significant reaction as opinion is divided over Jesus. Some follow him; others work ever harder to plot against him. More than that, as Caiaphas predicts, Jesus' forthcoming death is now becoming a reality. This reaction is not solely based on the miracle or sign that has preceded it. Rather it is because of the whole pattern of Jesus' ministry as it has unfolded.

This makes an important point to us as we encounter the narrative today. It is important because it asks us to reconsider everything that has gone before, to look closely at everything Jesus has said and done. As we do that, we may identify the words and deeds that have changed the perspective of people, whether that be towards faith or further away from it, as they become even more entrenched in tradition and the reinforcement of barriers.

Caiaphas clearly anticipates the chaos that could result from Jesus' ministry, and that fear of disorder is what gives rise to what seems like a fair exchange: one man's life for the life of the whole nation. Of course, what does happen is that Jesus' life was given for all – but for resurrection into new life allowing hope to shatter fear. At the end of this passage, we note how Jesus withdraws to the edges of the desert, and the scene is set for what will unfold.

> Gracious Father,
> you gave up your Son
> out of love for the world:
> lead us to ponder the mysteries of his passion,
> that we may know eternal peace
> through the shedding of our Saviour's blood,
> Jesus Christ our Lord.

*Reflection by* **Helen-Ann Hartley**     37

## Wednesday 5 April

Psalms **55**, 124 *or* **119.57-80**
Jeremiah 22.20 – 23.8
John 12.1-11

### John 12.1-11

*'The house was filled with the fragrance of the perfume' (v.3)*

While we are immediately drawn to the words on the page as we read this passage, this is a narrative that involves all the senses, and particularly the sense of smell. First, there is the meal that is served, which may have been a 'thank you' feast following the raising of Lazarus. The aromas of hospitality must have filled the place where Jesus ate.

More than that, however, an unexpected and outrageous gesture follows the meal when Mary anoints Jesus' feet. The amount of oil used would have been rightly seen as excessive. Indeed, John gives us the volume used, 'a pound', which is a extremely large amount. Undoubtedly it would have completely filled the house with perfume. We can almost smell it too. We hear Judas' words in verse 5, all the while knowing who the real disciple is here: Mary.

It is ironic too that Mary anoints Jesus for his burial, the one who gave new life to her brother. Mary's prophetic gesture is given sinister context by the renewed plot to kill Jesus, but not only that, to kill Lazarus too.

We might note also that a 'great crowd' is gathered (v.9), a form of ancient 'rubber-necking' as they stare at Lazarus. The perfume that lingers becomes bitter-sweet as the aroma of life is mixed with the stench of death.

COLLECT

Most merciful God,
who by the death and resurrection of your Son Jesus Christ
delivered and saved the world:
grant that by faith in him who suffered on the cross
we may triumph in the power of his victory;
through Jesus Christ your Son our Lord,
who is alive and reigns with you,
in the unity of the Holy Spirit,
one God, now and for ever.

| *Reflection by* **Helen-Ann Hartley**

Psalms **40**, 125 *or* 56, **57** (63\*)
Jeremiah 23.9-32
John 12.12-19

**Thursday 6 April**

## John 12.12-19
*'Look, the world has gone after him!' (v.19)*

Once, I waited for what seemed like eternity to catch a glimpse of a famous person. I was making my way through the city, but found myself stuck behind a gradually forming crowd of people. Being curious, I asked what was happening, and when I was told that the man in question might be going out for a run, I decided to stay and see if I could catch a glimpse. Eventually, he emerged from the hotel, with some security accompaniment and off they headed for their run. It was all over in an instant and afterwards, normality was resumed – as if nothing had happened at all.

Jesus' entry into Jerusalem presents a different picture. The Greek in verse 17 emphasizes more than the crowd's simple curiosity about Jesus; it stresses their *testimony* to Jesus and all that he had done. This is in turn highlighted by the observation of the Pharisees at the end of the passage. It wasn't a few people who followed Jesus; it seemed like the whole world.

Certainly Jesus generated a good deal of curiosity among people, but usually people are expected to do something in response, if not immediately then in the future. Faith begins in wonder, yet grows through knowledge and understanding. If we want the whole world to follow Jesus, then we have some explaining to do! Making Jesus known in word and in deed is the mandate for discipleship: that others may know and in turn share that good news with all whom they meet.

Gracious Father,
you gave up your Son
out of love for the world:
lead us to ponder the mysteries of his passion,
that we may know eternal peace
through the shedding of our Saviour's blood,
Jesus Christ our Lord.

COLLECT

**Friday 7 April**

### John 12.20-36*a*

*'Sir, we wish to see Jesus' (v.21)*

This request comes on the lips of 'some Greeks' (v.20), meaning some gentiles. Their presence in the story reminds us that Jesus' mission was universal; it links the previous complaint from the Pharisees about 'the whole world' coming to see Jesus with what happens next. Jesus' response gives a clear indication of the coming glory and its connection with the cost of discipleship. This is serious and hard to bear, and not only are our eyes directed to Jesus, but our ears are also overwhelmed with the sound of God's voice, which is described as thunder. The crowd fails to realize that this is for their own benefit, however, and their misunderstanding appears to persist, so once again Jesus talks about the theme of light and darkness. Jesus' passion takes us to a place of darkness, but we are children of light and share in that inheritance of the resurrection having happened, yet being always present in the hope we are called to bear to others.

It is significant that this passage begins with the request for sight of Jesus, so that they might believe. Seeing Jesus became a mark of apostleship, and this explains why Paul in his letters often proclaims boldly that he is an apostle because he has seen Jesus. The challenge for us, which is also an opportunity, is to show others the way to the deeper sight of the wisdom of God that is revealed in Christ for all time.

COLLECT

Most merciful God,
who by the death and resurrection of your Son Jesus Christ
delivered and saved the world:
grant that by faith in him who suffered on the cross
we may triumph in the power of his victory;
through Jesus Christ your Son our Lord,
who is alive and reigns with you,
in the unity of the Holy Spirit,
one God, now and for ever.

| *Reflection by* **Helen-Ann Hartley**

### John 12.36*b*-end

*'After Jesus had said this, he departed and hid from them' (v.36b)*

One of the constant themes of the fourth Gospel is the ongoing sense of things having been revealed and hidden. It's an uncomfortable notion, the idea that Jesus would deliberately hide from the crowds who have followed his every move with increasing devotion. What would your reaction be, I wonder, if the man you had begun to devote your life to suddenly disappeared? John's narrative explains why Jesus hid: the crowds did not believe in him. But wait? 'Of course we believe,' you hear the crowds implore. The reason provided indicates that unbelief – described in the very Johannine way as 'blindness' – is a part of God's plan. That sounds difficult to grasp. Yet again, we are forced into the position of reflecting hard on the quality of our faith. We believe, but do we really believe and trust in God?

Jesus points the way to God; it is not enough just to follow Jesus – there is more work to be done in our lives so that we might have eternal life. This points to more of a journey of faith that must be persevered with. It is life-long.

Here, at the end of Jesus' public ministry, the challenge is laid down. Will we always be in the darkness, or will we embrace the light and glory of God in our lives? What is hidden will be revealed, but we must help it to be so.

Gracious Father,
you gave up your Son
out of love for the world:
lead us to ponder the mysteries of his passion,
that we may know eternal peace
through the shedding of our Saviour's blood,
Jesus Christ our Lord.

COLLECT

## Monday 10 April

### Monday of Holy Week

### Luke 22.1-23

*'Then he took a cup …' (v.17)*

Today's reading seems to catapult us to Maundy Thursday three days early. Why are we reading about the Last Supper? The chronology seems all wrong.

Holy Week isn't simply a linear experience. We retrace the story of the passion and death of Christ while already knowing how it ends. Or, to put it more accurately, we are living with how the ending is unfolding. We relive the story of Holy Week to go more deeply into the meaning of the cross.

Christians live in an interim age. The acclamation frequently used at the end of many eucharistic prayers expresses it. 'Christ has died. Christ is risen. Christ will come again.' At the Last Supper, Jesus gave us the means of remembering him during this long period when we wait 'until the kingdom of God comes'. There's a lot yet to happen.

As part of an oral examination at Oxford, Oscar Wilde was asked to translate one of the gospels directly from the Greek. He was given the story of the Passion of Christ. He translated fluently. The examiners were satisfied, but he carried on translating. When they stopped him a second time, Oscar said: 'Do let me go on. I want to see how it ends.' We are still finding out.

COLLECT

Almighty and everlasting God,
who in your tender love towards the human race
    sent your Son our Saviour Jesus Christ
to take upon him our flesh
and to suffer death upon the cross:
grant that we may follow the example of his patience and humility,
and also be made partakers of his resurrection;
through Jesus Christ your Son our Lord,
who is alive and reigns with you,
in the unity of the Holy Spirit,
one God, now and for ever.

*Reflection by* **Graham James**

Psalm 27
Lamentations 3.1-18
Luke 22.[24-38] 39-53

### Luke 22.[24-38] 39-53

*'[Judas] approached Jesus to kiss him' (v.47)*

Auguste Rodin made three large-scale versions of his most famous sculpture *The Kiss*. The work is based on the story in Dante's *Inferno* of an Italian noblewoman who falls in love with her brother-in-law. Her husband kills both her and his brother. The sculpture depicts the lovers on the brink of a kiss that will destroy them. Nowadays we are more likely to observe the eroticism in the sculpture than the danger.

Our tendency to confine kisses to romance prompts us to think that Judas chose a particularly repellent means of betrayal. Yet it was commonplace in the ancient world for a pupil to greet his teacher with a kiss. Judas was doing nothing unusual except that he had brought armed soldiers with him. His kiss identified Jesus. We still speak of 'the kiss of death' acknowledging the way Judas' kiss has shaped our history and culture.

Jesus had not turned out as Judas expected. He was disappointed in him. We do not know precisely what Judas expected, but probably he longed for a greater display of power and authority from a messianic figure. Many people feel disappointed by God because their image of him isn't the one that the events of Holy Week reveal. Following Jesus is more dangerous than we think. The dangers often lie within ourselves. Do we realize it?

True and humble king,
hailed by the crowd as Messiah:
grant us the faith to know you and love you,
that we may be found beside you
on the way of the cross,
which is the path of glory.

COLLECT

## **Wednesday 12 April**

Wednesday of Holy Week

Psalm 102 [or 102.1-18]
Wisdom 1.16 – 2.1; 2.12-22
*or* Jeremiah 11.18-20
Luke 22.54-end

### Luke 22.54-end

*'The Lord turned and looked at Peter' (v.61)*

In Luke's Gospel we move very quickly from the betrayal of Judas to the denial of Peter. The cumulative impact on Jesus is ever greater isolation. It's accentuated in Luke's account of events in the High Priest's house since Jesus is near enough to overhear Peter's denial of him. No words are exchanged but 'the Lord turned and looked at Peter'.

Peter's regret is immediate. 'He went out and wept bitterly'. The tragic isolation of Jesus gets worse. He is then blindfolded and has to bear the mockery of the guards. They taunt him by saying that if he is a prophet, surely he will be able to say who is hitting him.

We leave Peter with his tears. They are tears of repentance. He hasn't run away in anger or justified his betrayal. He's ashamed of himself. In Luke's account of the Last Supper, Jesus says to Peter 'once you have turned back, strengthen your brothers' (Luke 22.32). Sometimes Peter seems a fractured rock on whom to build the Church. Perhaps the Church of Jesus Christ has to be built on someone who makes mistakes, repents and builds his life again. It was the American diplomat Edward Phelps who once said: 'The man who makes no mistakes does not usually make anything.' Have our mistakes shaped our discipleship more than we recognize?

COLLECT

Almighty and everlasting God,
who in your tender love towards the human race
    sent your Son our Saviour Jesus Christ
to take upon him our flesh
and to suffer death upon the cross:
grant that we may follow the example of his patience and humility,
and also be made partakers of his resurrection;
through Jesus Christ your Son our Lord,
who is alive and reigns with you,
in the unity of the Holy Spirit,
one God, now and for ever.

Psalms 42, 43
Leviticus 16.2-24
Luke 23.1-25

**Thursday 13 April**

Maundy Thursday

### Luke 23.1-25

*'... their voices prevailed' (v.23)*

Luke's account of the trial of Jesus does its best to exonerate Pontius Pilate. He finds Jesus innocent three times (vv.4,14,20), an intriguing parallel with Peter's threefold denial a chapter earlier. The voices of the people prevail. Pilate gives in to the popular demand that Jesus should be crucified.

There isn't much evidence from other sources that Pontius Pilate was a benign figure likely to be swayed by the local population. He was reputed to be a determined and unyielding Roman Governor for whom the voice of the people was to be silenced, not heeded.

It is the innocence of Jesus that is emphasized by Luke. 'Why, what evil has he done?' asks Pilate of the crowd, to which their only response is 'Crucify him'. In the light of later persecution, Luke the historian may be trying to show the Roman Empire that it has nothing to fear from Christianity. We are unlikely to read this without thinking of the many innocent victims of injustice and conflicts in our world today, and of the continuing persecution of Christians.

God's response to such injustice is to invite into his kingdom those who never thought they would have a place there. The promise of the kingdom passes to those who were not God's chosen people, to nations not even looking for the Messiah. Injustice does not have the last word.

True and humble king,
hailed by the crowd as Messiah:
grant us the faith to know you and love you,
that we may be found beside you
on the way of the cross,
which is the path of glory.

COLLECT

## Friday 14 April

### Good Friday

Psalm 69
Genesis 22.1-18
John 19.38-end
*or* Hebrews 10.1-10

### Hebrews 10.1-10

*'I have come to do your will' (v.9)*

The prophets of Israel challenged reliance on the rituals of sacrifice. 'I desire steadfast love and not sacrifice' (Hosea 6.6). But the will of God was not to do away with all sacrifice. There was to be one sacrifice – 'the offering of the body of Jesus Christ' – and those who had faith in Christ would be 'sanctified'.

The letter to the Hebrews requires a leap of imagination for those of us without much comprehension of ritual sacrifices. We know, however, that lovers will sacrifice their lives for those they love. Parents will often be willing to die to save their children. The concept of sacrifice is far from dead. Love, suffering and sacrifices go together.

In the autobiography of the famous crime novelist Agatha Christie, there is a striking passage. She's at school when a maths teacher launches into a speech about the Christian life: 'To be a Christian you must face and accept the life that Christ faced and lived; you must enjoy things as he enjoyed things ... but you must also know what it means ... to feel all your friends have forsaken you, that those you love and trust have turned away from you, and that God himself has forsaken you ... If you love you will suffer, and if you do not love you will not know the meaning of a Christian life.' The teacher then returned to the problems of compound interest. The compound interest of Christ's sacrifice on the cross makes this day Good Friday.

COLLECT

Almighty Father,
look with mercy on this your family
for which our Lord Jesus Christ was content to be betrayed
    and given up into the hands of sinners
    and to suffer death upon the cross;
who is alive and glorified with you and the Holy Spirit,
one God, now and for ever.

*Reflection by* **Graham James**

Psalm 142
Hosea 6.1-6
John 2.18-22

### John 2.18-22

*'… will you raise it up in three days?' (v.20)*

Today is Holy Saturday, or Easter Eve (definitely not Easter Saturday, whatever the media or even some errant churches say). A small army will spend hours today decorating churches, arranging flowers and building Easter gardens. Christians tend to avoid explicit remembrance of a day when Jesus stays dead.

Pope Pius XII wasn't known as a reforming Pope, but back in 1951 he introduced a major liturgical change. The ceremonies welcoming Christ's resurrection had crept ever earlier until they normally took place on Holy Saturday morning. Pius XII shifted them back to Saturday evening, since the evening is the biblical beginning of a new day (Genesis 1.5).

Jesus stays dead on Holy Saturday and rises on the third day. But why three days? There is the sign of Jonah who returned after three days in the belly of the whale, prefiguring the return of the Son of Man (Matthew 12.40). There is the prophecy of Hosea to be fulfilled – 'on the third day he will raise us up' (Hosea 6.2). In today's reading from John's Gospel, Jesus predicts his rising in three days, referring to the temple of his body. Some even speak of a Jewish tradition that the departed spirit stayed around the body for three days before moving on. This had to be real death that Jesus experienced. There is one certainty for everyone – death. Jesus has known death. Holy Saturday has an importance out of all proportion to our barren liturgical observance of it. We need to face the desolation of this sombre day – as Jesus did.

Grant, Lord,
that we who are baptized into the death
of your Son our Saviour Jesus Christ
may continually put to death our evil desires
and be buried with him;
and that through the grave and gate of death
we may pass to our joyful resurrection;
through his merits,
who died and was buried and rose again for us,
your Son Jesus Christ our Lord.

COLLECT

## Morning Prayer – a simple form

*Preparation*

O Lord, open our lips
**and our mouth shall proclaim your praise.**

A prayer of thanksgiving for Lent *(for Passiontide see p. 50)*

Blessed are you, Lord God of our salvation,
to you be glory and praise for ever.
In the darkness of our sin you have shone in our hearts
to give the light of the knowledge of the glory of God
in the face of Jesus Christ.
Open our eyes to acknowledge your presence,
that freed from the misery of sin and shame
we may grow into your likeness from glory to glory.
Blessed be God, Father, Son and Holy Spirit.
**Blessed be God for ever.**

*Word of God*

Psalmody *(the psalm or psalms listed for the day)*

**Glory to the Father and to the Son
and to the Holy Spirit;
as it was in the beginning is now:
and shall be for ever. Amen.**

Reading from Holy Scripture *(one or both of the passages set for the day)*

Reflection

The Benedictus (The Song of Zechariah) *(see opposite page)*

*Prayers*

Intercessions – a time of prayer for the day and its tasks, the world and its need, the church and her life.

The Collect for the Day

The Lord's Prayer *(see p. 51)*

*Conclusion*

A blessing or the Grace *(see p. 51)*, or a concluding response

Let us bless the Lord
**Thanks be to God**

### Benedictus (The Song of Zechariah)

1    Blessed be the Lord the God of Israel, ♦
     who has come to his people and set them free.

2    He has raised up for us a mighty Saviour, ♦
     born of the house of his servant David.

3    Through his holy prophets God promised of old ♦
     to save us from our enemies,
        from the hands of all that hate us,

4    To show mercy to our ancestors, ♦
     and to remember his holy covenant.

5    This was the oath God swore to our father Abraham: ♦
     to set us free from the hands of our enemies,

6    Free to worship him without fear, ♦
     holy and righteous in his sight
        all the days of our life.

7    And you, child, shall be called the prophet of the Most High, ♦
     for you will go before the Lord to prepare his way,

8    To give his people knowledge of salvation ♦
     by the forgiveness of all their sins.

9    In the tender compassion of our God ♦
     the dawn from on high shall break upon us,

10   To shine on those who dwell in darkness
        and the shadow of death, ♦
     and to guide our feet into the way of peace.

*Luke 1.68-79*

**Glory to the Father and to the Son
and to the Holy Spirit;
as it was in the beginning is now:
and shall be for ever. Amen.**

## Seasonal Prayers of Thanksgiving

*Passiontide*

Blessed are you, Lord God of our salvation,
to you be praise and glory for ever.
As a man of sorrows and acquainted with grief
your only Son was lifted up
that he might draw the whole world to himself.
May we walk this day in the way of the cross
and always be ready to share its weight,
declaring your love for all the world.
Blessed be God, Father, Son and Holy Spirit.
**Blessed be God for ever.**

*At Any Time*

Blessed are you, creator of all,
to you be praise and glory for ever.
As your dawn renews the face of the earth
bringing light and life to all creation,
may we rejoice in this day you have made;
as we wake refreshed from the depths of sleep,
open our eyes to behold your presence
and strengthen our hands to do your will,
that the world may rejoice and give you praise.
Blessed be God, Father, Son and Holy Spirit.
**Blessed be God for ever.**

*after Lancelot Andrewes (1626)*

## The Lord's Prayer and The Grace

---

Our Father in heaven,
hallowed be your name,
your kingdom come,
your will be done,
on earth as in heaven.
Give us today our daily bread.
Forgive us our sins
as we forgive those who sin against us.
Lead us not into temptation
but deliver us from evil.
For the kingdom, the power,
and the glory are yours
now and for ever.
Amen.

*(or)*

Our Father, who art in heaven,
hallowed be thy name;
thy kingdom come;
thy will be done;
on earth as it is in heaven.
Give us this day our daily bread.
And forgive us our trespasses,
as we forgive those who trespass against us.
And lead us not into temptation;
but deliver us from evil.
For thine is the kingdom,
the power and the glory,
for ever and ever.
Amen.

---

The grace of our Lord Jesus Christ,
and the love of God,
and the fellowship of the Holy Spirit,
be with us all evermore.
Amen.

# An Order for Night Prayer (Compline)

The Lord almighty grant us a quiet night and a perfect end.
**Amen.**

Our help is in the name of the Lord
**who made heaven and earth.**

*A period of silence for reflection on the past day may follow.*

*The following or other suitable words of penitence may be used*

**Most merciful God,
we confess to you,
before the whole company of heaven and one another,
that we have sinned in thought, word and deed
and in what we have failed to do.
Forgive us our sins,
heal us by your Spirit
and raise us to new life in Christ. Amen.**

O God, make speed to save us.
**O Lord, make haste to help us.**

**Glory to the Father and to the Son
and to the Holy Spirit;
as it was in the beginning is now
and shall be for ever. Amen.
Alleluia.**

*The following or another suitable hymn may be sung*

Before the ending of the day,
Creator of the world, we pray
That you, with steadfast love, would keep
Your watch around us while we sleep.

From evil dreams defend our sight,
From fears and terrors of the night;
Tread underfoot our deadly foe
That we no sinful thought may know.

O Father, that we ask be done
Through Jesus Christ, your only Son;
And Holy Spirit, by whose breath
Our souls are raised to life from death.

# The Word of God

*Psalmody*

*One or more of Psalms 4, 91 or 134 may be used.*

*Psalm 134*

1   Come, bless the Lord, all you servants of the Lord, ✦
     you that by night stand in the house of the Lord.

2   Lift up your hands towards the sanctuary ✦
     and bless the Lord.

3   The Lord who made heaven and earth ✦
     give you blessing out of Zion.

**Glory to the Father and to the Son
and to the Holy Spirit;
as it was in the beginning is now
and shall be for ever. Amen.**

*Scripture Reading*

*One of the following short lessons or another suitable
passage is read*

You, O Lord, are in the midst of us and we are called by your
name; leave us not, O Lord our God.

*Jeremiah 14.9*

*(or)*

Be sober, be vigilant, because your adversary the devil is
prowling round like a roaring lion, seeking for someone
to devour. Resist him, strong in the faith.

*1 Peter 5.8,9*

*(or)*

The servants of the Lamb shall see the face of God, whose name
will be on their foreheads. There will be no more night: they will
not need the light of a lamp or the light of the sun, for God will
be their light, and they will reign for ever and ever.

*Revelation 22.4,5*

*The following responsory may be said*

Into your hands, O Lord, I commend my spirit.
**Into your hands, O Lord, I commend my spirit.**
For you have redeemed me, Lord God of truth.
**I commend my spirit.**
Glory to the Father and to the Son
and to the Holy Spirit.
**Into your hands, O Lord, I commend my spirit.**

*Or, in Easter*

Into your hands, O Lord, I commend my spirit.
    Alleluia, alleluia.
**Into your hands, O Lord, I commend my spirit.**
    **Alleluia, alleluia.**
For you have redeemed me, Lord God of truth.
**Alleluia, alleluia.**
Glory to the Father and to the Son
and to the Holy Spirit.
**Into your hands, O Lord, I commend my spirit.**
    **Alleluia, alleluia.**

Keep me as the apple of your eye.
**Hide me under the shadow of your wings.**

*Gospel Canticle*

*Nunc Dimittis (The Song of Simeon)*

**Save us, O Lord, while waking,**
**and guard us while sleeping,**
**that awake we may watch with Christ**
**and asleep may rest in peace.**

1    Now, Lord, you let your servant go in peace:
     your word has been fulfilled.

2    My own eyes have seen the salvation
     which you have prepared in the sight of every people;

3    A light to reveal you to the nations
     and the glory of your people Israel.

*Luke 2.29-32*

**Glory to the Father and to the Son**
**and to the Holy Spirit;**
**as it was in the beginning is now**
**and shall be for ever. Amen.**

**Save us, O Lord, while waking,**
**and guard us while sleeping,**
**that awake we may watch with Christ**
**and asleep may rest in peace.**

# Prayers

*Intercessions and thanksgivings may be offered here.*

*The Collect*

Visit this place, O Lord, we pray,
and drive far from it the snares of the enemy;
may your holy angels dwell with us and guard us in peace,
and may your blessing be always upon us;
through Jesus Christ our Lord.
**Amen.**

*The Lord's Prayer (see p. 51) may be said.*

# The Conclusion

In peace we will lie down and sleep;
**for you alone, Lord, make us dwell in safety.**

Abide with us, Lord Jesus,
**for the night is at hand and the day is now past.**

As the night watch looks for the morning,
**so do we look for you, O Christ.**

[Come with the dawning of the day
**and make yourself known in the breaking of the bread.**]

The Lord bless us and watch over us;
the Lord make his face shine upon us and be gracious to us;
the Lord look kindly on us and give us peace.
**Amen.**

# Love what you've read?

Why not consider using *Reflections for Daily Prayer* all year round? We also publish these meditations on Bible readings in an annual format, containing material for the entire Church year.

The volume for 2017/18 will mark 10 years of the highly successful *Reflections* series. Published in May 2017, it features contributions from a host of distinguished writers: Christopher Cocksworth, Gillian Cooper, Stephen Cottrell, Steven Croft, Maggi Dawn, Malcolm Guite, Christopher Herbert, John Kiddle, Barbara Mosse, Mark Oakley, Martyn Percy, John Pritchard, Ben Quash, Angela Tilby, Catherine Williams, Jane Williams, Lucy Winkett, Christopher Woods and Jeremy Worthen.

**Reflections for Daily Prayer:**
**Advent 2017 to the eve of Advent 2018**

ISBN 978 1 78140 019 7
**£16.99** • Available May 2017

## Can't wait for next year?

You can still pick up this year's edition of *Reflections*, direct from us (at **www.chpublishing.co.uk**) or from your local Christian bookshop.

**Reflections for Daily Prayer:**
**Advent 2016 to the eve of Advent 2017**

ISBN 978 0 7151 4715 3
**£16.99** • Available Now

# REFLECTIONS FOR DAILY PRAYER

## App

Make Bible study and reflection a part of your routine wherever you go with the Reflections for Daily Prayer App for Apple and Android devices.

Download the app for free from the App Store (Apple devices) or Google Play (Android devices) and receive a week's worth of reflections free. Then purchase a monthly, three-monthly or annual subscription to receive up-to-date content.

# REFLECTIONS FOR SUNDAYS (YEAR A)

*Reflections for Sundays* offers over 250 reflections on the Principal Readings for every Sunday and major Holy Day in Year A, from the same experienced team of writers that have made *Reflections for Daily Prayer* so successful. For each Sunday and major Holy Day, they provide:

- full lectionary details for the Principal Service
- a reflection on each Old Testament reading (both Continuous and Related)
- a reflection on the Epistle
- a reflection on the Gospel.

This book also contains a substantial introduction to the Gospel of Matthew, written by Paula Gooder.

**£14.99** • 288 pages
ISBN 978 0 7151 4735 1

Also available in Kindle and epub formats

# REFLECTIONS ON THE PSALMS

**£14.99** • 192 pages
ISBN 978 0 7151 4490 9

*Reflections on the Psalms* provides original and insightful meditations on each of the Bible's 150 Psalms.

Each reflection is accompanied by its corresponding Psalm refrain and prayer from the *Common Worship Psalter*, making this a valuable resource for personal or devotional use.

Specially written introductions by Paula Gooder and Steven Croft explore the Psalms and the Bible and the Psalms in the life of the Church.

# ENRICHING YOUR DAILY PRAYER

*Reflections for Lent* **is designed to enhance your spiritual journey through the season of Lent from Ash Wednesday to Holy Saturday.**

Covering Monday to Saturday each week, it offers stimulating and accessible reflections, from four respected Christian authors, on a reading selected from the Common Worship Weekday Lectionary.

Each day includes:

- **Full lectionary details for Morning Prayer**
- **A reflection on one of the Bible readings**
- **A Collect for the day**

This volume offers daily material taken from the *Reflections for Daily Prayer 2016/17* annual edition. It is ideal for individuals and groups seeking a simple yet profound daily prayer companion throughout Lent.

This book also contains:

- **A simple form of Morning Prayer** for Lent and Passiontide
- **A short form of Night Prayer** (also known as **Compline**)
- **An introduction to Lent** by Samuel Wells
- **A guide to the practice of daily prayer** by John Pritchard
- **A simple introduction to contemplative reading** of the Bible from Stephen Cottrell

**Also available in Kindle and epub formats.**

CHURCH HOUSE
PUBLISHING

www.chpublishing.co.uk

£4.99

ISBN 978-1-78140-004-3

9 781781 400043

Cover design: **Hugh Hillyard-Parker**